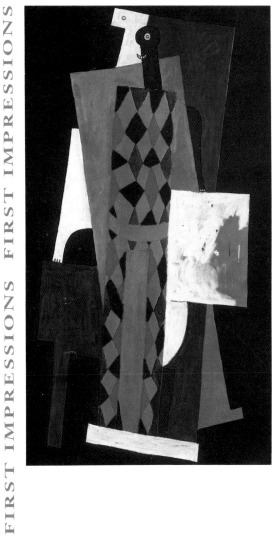

JOHN BEARDSLEY FIRST IMPRESSIONS

Pablo Picasso

HARRY N. ABRAMS, INC., PUBLISHERS, NEW YORK

SERIES EDITOR: Robert Morton
EDITOR: Ellyn Childs Allison
DESIGNER: Joan Lockhart
PHOTO RESEARCH: Johanna Cypis

Library of Congress Cataloging-in-Publication Data

Beardsley, John.
  Pablo Picasso / John Beardsley.
      p.   cm. — (First impressions)
  Includes index.
  Summary: Examines the life and work of Picasso, discussing how
and why his art looks the way it does and how it relates to the artist.
  ISBN 0-8109-3713-1
  1. Picasso, Pablo, 1881–1973—Juvenile literature.   2. Artists—
France—Biography—Juvenile literature.   [1. Picasso, Pablo,
1881–1973.   2. Artists.   3. Painting, French.   4. Painting,
Modern—20th century—France.   5. Art appreciation.]   I. Title.
II. Series: First impressions (New York, N.Y.)
N6853.P5B43   1991
709′.2—dc20
[B]   91-7741
                                                                    CIP

Text copyright © 1991 John Beardsley
Illustrations copyright © 1991 Harry N. Abrams, Inc.

Published in 1991 by Harry N. Abrams, Incorporated, New York
A Times Mirror Company

Printed and bound in Hong Kong

"MATERIALIZING A DREAM"

1 *METAMORPHOSIS.* THIS WORD MAY BE THE KEY TO UNDERSTANDING both the life and the art of Pablo Picasso. It signifies the capacity of a living organism to transform itself completely: a tadpole into a frog, for example, or a lowly caterpillar into an exquisite butterfly. Picasso was a master of metamorphosis. Looking at the remarkable quantity and quality of the paintings, sculptures, drawings, prints, and ceramics he produced during his long life, we can see that he was one of the most extraordinary artists who ever lived. Reading the accounts of the people who knew him, we also know that he was a fascinating, appealing, passionate, and sometimes difficult man.

But what set Picasso apart from other artists was his capacity to change. Most artists find a style or a technique they are good at, and stick to it. Not Picasso. He was constantly transforming his art, moving from style to style with ease. At times he painted the most realistic pictures, making every-

PAINTER WITH MODEL KNITTING. *1931. In this witty etching, made as an illustration for a novel, Picasso shows the two sides of his artistic nature — realism and abstraction.*

6

day objects look just as they are. But at others, he transformed and distorted the things he saw, tearing them apart so we can barely recognize them.

Picasso seemed to be several artists at once, all of them self-confident. Always he was true to his own vision, no matter how difficult or strange his work looked to other people. If in the same year, or even at the same time, he painted in two very different styles, that was because he always chose the style that seemed right for the subject. He once said, "It is my misfortune— and probably my delight—to use things as my passions tell me.... The

SELF-PORTRAIT. *1901.*

things—so much the worse for them; they just have to put up with it."

Picasso's self-confidence led him a long way from traditional painting. He was brought up to believe that a painting should be something of beauty, something instructive, and something that gives an accurate picture of outward reality. But he wanted something else from his art and didn't hesitate to reject the traditional standards, or canons, of art to achieve what he was after. "Art is not the application of a canon of beauty," he said in 1935, "but what the instinct and the brain can conceive beyond any canon."

Above all, he wanted his art to express the dreams, the emotions, and the visions of the artist. "It would be very interesting," he thought, "to preserve photographically . . . the metamorphoses of a picture. Possibly one might then discover the path followed by the brain in materializing a dream." Picasso thought of his art as the visible expression of his innermost mind, his heart, and his soul, with the possibility of infinite variety. "A painter paints to unload himself of feelings and visions," he said.

Picasso was a master of metamorphosis not only within his own art, however. He also transformed completely the work of the artists who followed him in this century. It may be that no other artist in history has so changed the look of

SELF-PORTRAIT. *1896. One of Picasso's first self-portraits was painted when he was only about fifteen years old.*

art. Because he worked in so many styles and materials and touched on so many themes in the course of his long life, he opened paths for other artists. Painters and sculptors are still developing ideas that Picasso first expressed.

Perhaps the best known of these new paths is the style called cubism, which Picasso developed with his friend Georges Braque. Cubism was one of the most important turns taken on the road toward abstract art, which has dominated the art of our time. Although Picasso himself never painted a fully abstract picture, cubism asserted that painting did not need to show us the things we could already see but could be a window into another world.

Picasso the man was as capable of metamorphosis as Picasso the artist. He was lively and charming, funny and imaginative, but also moody and stubborn, and occasionally cruel. This artist who could do anything, who was larger than life, was in fact short and compact, though powerfully built. His hands were small and fine. In his youth, he wore his dark hair swept across his wide brow, past slightly protruding ears. His handsome facial features were dominated by powerful black eyes that, as his friends recalled, seemed to see beneath the surface of things, laying open what was inside.

Picasso, so modern in his art and in his manner of living, was ancient in some ways. He was fascinated by age-old myths and rituals. He drew and painted the creatures of Greek legends and loved the spectacle of the bull-fight. He abandoned tradition in his personal life, observing neither the conventions of family nor any religion. But his friends remember that he was deeply superstitious. His companion for many years, Françoise Gilot, remembers that he would never allow her to lay his hat on the bed, for fear that someone would die within the next year. When she opened an umbrella in

■

SELF-PORTRAIT. *1901. At twenty,*
the sensitive and self-aware artist was already a master of his art.

the house, he insisted that they march around the room, third finger of each hand crossed over the index finger, waving their arms and shouting "Lagarto! Lagarto!" to chase bad luck away.

Picasso could never bear to throw anything away, and his living quarters were always filling up with treasures that others saw as junk. He had constant fears for his health. Throughout his life, he also suffered from deep and prolonged bouts of depression, which made him unable to rise from bed in the morning. At such times, nothing could cheer him, but he would finally get up and get to work. "He has never really lived for anything else but his art," recalled Fernande Olivier, his companion in early life. "This rather sad, sarcastic man . . . has not so much consoled himself—for he seemed always to be weighed down by some great sorrow—as forgotten himself in his work, and his love for it."

Picasso's complicated character revealed itself most forcefully in his relationships with women. He loved women—he did many beautiful paintings and drawings that show this. But he could also be hostile and manipulative toward them. For all the beautiful representations of women in his art, there are also horrifying ones that show women as frightening, demonic creatures.

In all, it may be that Picasso was like one or another of the creatures he loved to paint: the bull for example, or the Minotaur, that creature of legend who was half bull and half man. Like these creatures, he was headstrong and powerful. Like the Minotaur, to whom the youth of ancient Athens were periodically sent as offerings, he seemed to require that other personalities, especially those of the women in his life, be sacrificed to him. None of this takes away from the importance of Picasso the artist. But we sometimes think that because someone is a great artist they must be perfect as a person as well. Picasso reminds us that even genius takes a human form.

At times, Picasso could be humble. Although he was always serious about his art, he knew it was not the only thing of significance in the world. "If only [people] would realize above all," he said, "that an artist works of necessity, that he himself is only a trifling bit of the world, and that no more importance should be attached to him than to plenty of other things that please us in the world, though we can't explain them."

Picasso knew that the metamorphoses in his life and his art might seem too many and too difficult to follow. He cautioned against worrying too much about understanding every subject, every symbol, every game or invention in his art. "Everyone wants to understand art," he said. "Why not try to understand the songs of a bird? Why does one love the night, flowers, everything around one, without trying to understand them?" He knew that making too much effort to understand art could take away some of its magic.

Picasso was right about this. What we still prize about his art, what will make it appealing always, is the way it combines the things we know and understand with the things that escape our comprehension—the way it takes things of this world and transforms them into products of an artist's vision and imagination. The way, in short, that it materializes a dream.

■

SELF-PORTRAIT WITH A PALETTE. *(Detail). 1906.*
His earlier self-portraits
were more realistic,
but here Picasso distorts
his features for artistic effect.

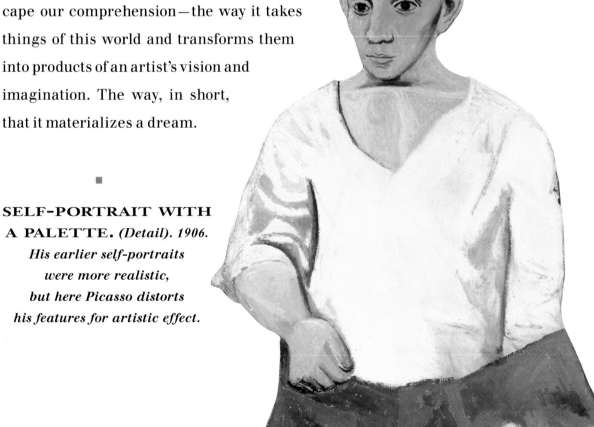

SELF-PORTRAIT. *1907. This painting suggests
how greatly Picasso would transform the image of the human face
as he developed the style known as cubism.*

THE YOUNG PICASSO

2 IT WAS NOT A PROMISING START. ON THE NIGHT OF OCTOBER 25, 1881, in the port city of Malaga in the south of Spain, a son was born to Doña Maria Picasso and Don José Ruiz Blasco. But the child was not breathing and appeared to be dead, so the midwife who was assisting at the birth set him aside to attend to the mother. An uncle, who was trained in medicine, saved the boy from suffocation.

Soon the boy who cheated death was christened Pablo Ruiz Picasso. In the customary Spanish way, his first name was followed by his father's family name, then his mother's. His father, a painter, was not at all the rebellious or bohemian artist that his son would become. He painted very traditional landscapes and still lifes of birds and flowers in the style favored by the academies, or official schools, of art. He also took his family responsibilities very seriously, taking care of his four unmarried sisters as well as his own wife and child. To make ends meet, he took two jobs, one as a teacher in the local school of fine arts, the other as curator, or caretaker of the collection, at the municipal museum.

Picasso, at about the age of eight, with his sister Lola

Don José's responsibilities continued to grow: Pablo was the first of three children born to him and Doña Maria. In 1884, a sister named Lola was born, also under difficult circumstances. She came into the world in the apartment of her parents' friends, where the family had taken refuge during an earthquake. A second daughter, Concep-

The drawing of Picasso when he was about 21 was made by Ramón Casas, a friend and compatriot at Barcelona's café Els Quatre Gats (The Four Cats).

■

ción, was born in 1887; she would die of diphtheria at an early age.

Pablo would prove to be an extraordinary child, as far as art was concerned. It is said that he learned to draw long before he could talk. When he did learn to speak, his first word was "piz, piz," an urgent request for *lápiz,* a pencil. He watched his father paint, and years later could remember the look of his realistic pictures.

But the young child was even more receptive to the sights of his native Malaga. The bullfights, the religious processions, the slums with their gypsies, the sun-baked landscape with its rocky promontories and fortress castles—these images would turn up again and again in his art in later years. The bullfight in particular would fascinate Picasso for the whole of his long life. First came a spectacular parade. Then came the fight itself, distinguished by festive costumes and elaborate displays of combat between the bull and the bullfighter, or torero, who fought first on horseback and then on foot. It may be that Picasso later saw in the torero's courageous artistry and his triumph over death something that would inspire his own life as a creator.

When Pablo was ten, his father took a position as art master at a secondary school in La Coruña, on the Atlantic coast in the far northwest corner of Spain. It was not a happy move for his father—Don José had not wanted to leave Malaga but was forced to do so to support his family. Moreover, he did not like the frequent rain and fog of his new home, which caused a gloom in the family only deepened by the death there of Concepción.

For Pablo, however, the move was a great opportunity. Since he disliked school and would never be good at academic subjects like mathematics, he was allowed by the school to spend much of his time learning to draw and paint from his father. He quickly mastered making charcoal drawings, copying the plaster casts of statues which every traditional school kept in those days. Impressed by his talent, Don José would often leave paintings for his son to finish.

The story is told that on one such occasion near the end of four years in La Coruña, Don José left Pablo to

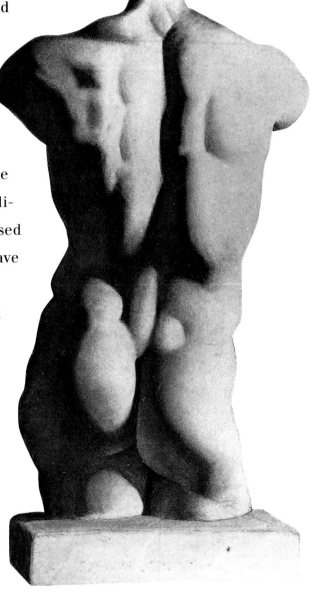

STUDY OF A CAST OF A CLASSICAL SCULPTURE.
About 1893. By the time he was twelve, Picasso had already acquired the precise, realistic drawing skills taught at the art academies.

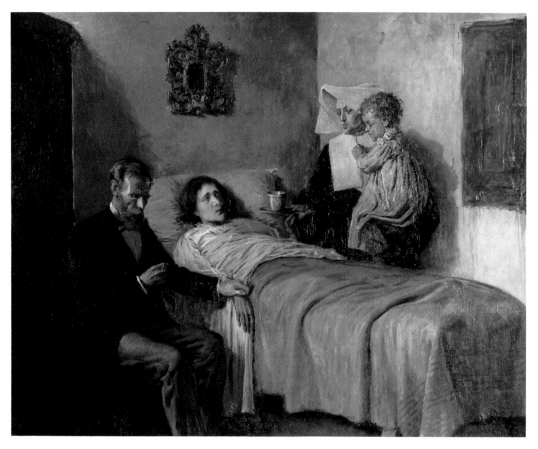

SCIENCE AND CHARITY. *1897. For this painting,*
an allegory in which a doctor represents Science and a nun stands for Charity,
Picasso's father helped him choose the subject and posed as the doctor.

complete a painting of pigeons. On his return, he found the pigeons not only finished but finished so realistically that he surrendered his brushes, paints, and palette to his son. He declared that Pablo's talent was already greater than his own and that he would never paint again.

This story is a fable, but it contains an element of truth: the thirteen-year-old artist was becoming a master in his own right. Yet his talent must have made him feel conflicted and guilty as well, for he was overtaking his father in his own profession. This must have opened the emotional distance between father and son. Already, they were physically different. Pablo had grown to resemble his mother—short and intense, with dark eyes and black hair—whereas his father was tall, thin, and red-haired.

Again, it may be that in this youthful conflict with his father there was something of crucial importance in the life of Picasso the artist. Feeling both proud and guilty of his accomplishment, he would want, on the one hand, to show it, on the other, to hide it. All his life, Picasso seemed to follow this pattern. He would master one style, then quickly replace it with another, as if he were both proud and ashamed of his achievement.

In the summer of 1895, life improved for Don José. He received a teaching position at the Barcelona academy of fine arts. Although Barcelona is also in the north of Spain, far from Malaga, it is on the opposite coast from La Coruña. It is on the sunny Mediterranean side, near the border with France. Moreover, it is a center of commerce and culture, and at the turn of the century was home to many of the most interesting artists in Spain.

It was in Barcelona that Picasso's life as an artist really began. Arriving there at age fourteen, he enrolled in the academy. Because he had received previous training from his father, he was allowed to skip the introductory course—drawing antique sculptures—which he had already mastered. He proceeded directly to the examination for the advanced class, in which he would draw and paint from a live model. Students were permitted a month to complete this examination, in which

MAN WITH A CAP. *(Detail). 1895.*
Picasso painted the study of a beggar in La Coruña.

time they had to demonstrate some skill at drawing the human figure. Picasso finished it in one day.

The academy could not long hold Picasso's interest. By the summer of 1896, Don José found him a studio, his first, where he could work more independently. He shared the studio with Manuel Pallarés, whom he had met at the academy and with whom he would remain friendly all his life. Under his father's guidance, he painted subjects that were considered appropriate and acceptable by the academy, such as the visit of a doctor to a dying woman, a first communion, and a choirboy.

Picasso spent the summer of 1897 in Malaga, and then left for Madrid that autumn. Just sixteen, Picasso was away from home and family for the first time, living in a city he had only visited briefly once before. He found modest

lodgings and enrolled in the city's imposing art school, the Royal Academy of San Fernando, passing his entrance examinations with the same speed and skill he had shown in Barcelona. But this academy too would soon bore Picasso. He found the streets and cafés, the gypsies and circus performers, the dogs and horses of much more interest. Picasso lived in poverty,

■

DESIGN FOR A CARNIVAL POSTER. *1899. Picasso loved entertainments like the carnival, the bullfight, and the circus, as a quick sketch reveals.*

20

LE MOULIN DE LA GALETTE. *1900. Brushed in a loose, impressionistic style, this is the most important painting that resulted from Picasso's first visit to Paris.*

and after a winter of hunger and cold, he fell ill with scarlet fever and returned to his family in Barcelona in the spring of 1898.

By June, he was well enough to leave Barcelona with his friend Manuel Pallarés. Together they went to Pallarés's home in Horta de San Juan (also called Horta de Ebro), a village of stone houses crowded around a church in the nearby region called Aragon. It was Picasso's introduction to the countryside and rural people. He felt the same kind of bond with them as he did with the ordinary working people of the city, and images of laboring and resting peasants began to appear in his sketchbooks. He and Pallarés also spent time living in a cave high in the mountains above Horta, where Picasso drew some of his first landscapes.

In the spring of 1899, Picasso returned to Barcelona. This time, he found his own world there. It centered on the new café and cabaret Els Quatre Gats (The Four Cats). Founded in 1897 and modeled after a Parisian café, it was the gathering place of the leading artists, poets, and writers in Barcelona in the final years of the nineteenth century. But these were not artists who abided by the conservative standards of the art academies. They were the painters and poets of the modern age, who wanted art to express the life around them. Rather than taking their subjects from history or religion, they took them from the streets. Their art showed compassion for the poor and suggested that society must change to make their lives better.

Picasso spent a great deal of time at Els Quatre Gats, drawing portraits of his friends and sketches of the café interior to decorate its menus. He even had his first real exhibition there, in February 1900. Among those whom Picasso befriended at Els Quatre Gats was the poet Jaime Sabartés, who would in later years become his secretary. Another new acquaintance was a painter named Carlos Casagemas. Picasso and Casagemas shared a studio for a time, a whitewashed room that they could not afford to furnish. So Picasso painted the walls with everything they wanted. Tables and easy chairs appeared. So did a bookcase full of rare volumes. Flowers and fruit covered a sideboard on which coins had been carelessly scattered. A maid and a page stood waiting for orders.

But Picasso and Casagemas soon left all this pretend splendor behind. Both artists felt the pull of Paris, which was already the center of the new spirit in art. Casagemas had a little money, which would help get them there.

THE OLD GUITARIST. *1903. The melancholy mood and the dominant color of the painting show why it belongs to what is called Picasso's Blue Period.*

Picasso secured his parents' permission to go, promising that he would be back by Christmas. So in the fall of 1900, Picasso, just then celebrating his nineteenth birthday, set out with Casagemas on his first visit to Paris. Though he did not know it at the time, it would become his true home.

When Picasso and Casagemas arrived in Paris, they headed directly for Montmartre, then a remote district on a hilltop overlooking the center of Paris. It was already known as a neighborhood of artists and was the home of several other Spanish painters and sculptors who had moved to the city. Picasso quickly came to know the cafés and dance halls of Montmartre and paid visits to the museums and galleries of Paris as well. There he saw for the first time the work of painters such as Edgar Degas, Pierre-Auguste Renoir, Vincent van Gogh, and Henri de Toulouse-Lautrec.

Although he already knew something of their impressionistic style, this was an opportunity to learn it firsthand. These artists painted not with crisp outlines and sharp detail, but in a looser, more suggestive way. Through the free use of color, shimmering effects of light, and the hint of atmosphere — smoke, mist, or distant haze — they sought to convey their visual impressions of the world, not dispassionate, factual descriptions of it.

As usual, Picasso mastered this new style quickly. The painting *Le Moulin de la Galette,* apparently the first he did in Paris, shows the dusky, crowded interior of a dance hall, done in a sketchy style. Light flickers from gas lamps and reflects off the top hats of the men and the gowns of the women. In the darkness and the haze, we see only a suggestion of faces, hats, and figures.

Picasso's first visit to Paris wasn't long, however. He and Casagemas were back in Spain by the end of the year. Picasso later recalled that they went to Malaga because Casagemas had fallen in love with a woman in Paris who showed no interest in him, and Picasso thought the Mediterranean sun would cure his friend of his heartsickness. Within two weeks, however,

Picasso left for Madrid, where he remained through the spring of 1901. With a friend, he started a modern-art review there called *Arte Joven* (*Young Art*), with Picasso acting as art editor and illustrator.

It was about this time that Picasso stopped using his father's surname when he signed his pictures, and used only his mother's. Picasso is a less common name than Ruiz, and it must have appealed to the artist for that reason. But dropping his father's name may have had some emotional importance as well. It may have been a sign of the increasing artistic independence that Picasso was then feeling from his father.

When *Arte Joven* failed for lack of money, Picasso returned to Barcelona. But Paris beckoned to him. Nothing in Spain could compare with the artistic life of Paris. It was there that the most serious and advanced art was being made, there that art was being remade for the modern age. Picasso wanted to be there, too, to learn from and to test himself against the best. So in the spring of 1901 he left again for the north.

Whatever his hopes may have been, Picasso was not an instant success. In June of that year, he had his first exhibition in Paris, with the dealer Ambroise Vollard, friend and supporter of many of the best-known Parisian artists of the time, including Paul Cézanne, Degas, Renoir, and Auguste Rodin. Despite Vollard's enthusiasm for Picasso's work, nothing sold, and most reviews were negative. Picasso was criticized for painting too much like the impressionists.

By the end of the year, however, that was no longer the case. In the first of his many artistic metamorphoses, Picasso developed a much more personal style. He moved into his Blue Period, so-called because many of his paintings made during the next three years were almost entirely painted in different shades of blue. Typically, their subjects are poor mothers and children, blind old men, and beggars—melancholy themes that are in har-

LA VIE (LIFE). *1903.*
One of the largest and most ambitious of Picasso's Blue Period paintings, La Vie *suggests his feelings about the hardships suffered by some families.*

■

mony with the deep blue tones. These figures take up a large part of the canvas and are presented against plain backgrounds.

While there is no simple explanation for the melancholy feeling of these paintings, they are an indication of the difficulties that Picasso was experiencing at the time. Because he was not a quick success, he was no stranger to poverty, hunger, and cold. Moreover, the paintings show that Picasso was capable of feeling great sympathy for others who were experiencing the same difficulties. Picasso had another reason to be distressed: his friend Casagemas had returned to Paris earlier in the year and, unable to pull himself out of his depression, had committed suicide. Picasso memorialized his friend in a large painting called *Evocation* or *The Burial of Casagemas.* Death, like poverty, was haunting Picasso.

Perhaps in an effort to escape the gloom and chill of the Paris winter, Picasso returned to Barcelona early in 1902. There he continued to paint in the style of the Blue Period, but quickly he became restless. That fall, he returned to Paris and eventually moved into the one-room apartment of the poet Max Jacob, who had befriended him during his exhibition at

Vollard's gallery. Jacob had little more than Picasso, but what he had he shared. The two had to make do with a single bed: Jacob worked in a department store during the day while Picasso slept; Picasso worked or prowled the cafés and cabarets by night while Jacob slept. They had little food, and Picasso sold very little work, despite two exhibitions that year at the gallery of Berthe Weill. When winter came, they even resorted to burning a great pile of Picasso's drawings one night in a futile effort to keep warm.

Matters grew even worse when Jacob lost his job. So for a third time, in January 1903, Picasso returned to Barcelona, where he shared a studio with a friend. This time, he would remain in Spain for over a year and create some of the most important of the Blue Period paintings. Among them are compositions called *The Old Guitarist* and *The Blind Man's Meal.*

One of the most ambitious and puzzling paintings of this year is called *La Vie (Life)*. It shows a naked woman leaning against a nearly naked man, who gestures toward a fully clothed woman holding a child. Behind the figures are two paintings within the painting, sketches of crouching and embracing figures that are shown as if in a studio. In a drawing that Picasso made as a study for this painting, the male figure bears the face of Picasso. In the final painting, the face is that of Casagemas.

La Vie is difficult to interpret, but it seems to be an allegory of the life of the artist. It suggests that Picasso felt romantic love and love of family were different, even mutually exclusive. In fact, the painting would turn out to be strangely prophetic of Picasso's own life. He was never able to have a family in the usual sense. Again and again, he would leave women behind, even those to whom he was married or with whom he had children. He would find a replacement in a younger woman, who would become his new source of romantic and artistic inspiration. This habit was extremely painful for his partners, as is suggested by the figures in *La Vie*. Most vivid is the combination of sorrow and anger shown in the face of the mother.

Although Picasso's stay in Barcelona was productive, Paris had gotten into his blood. He would never lose his Spanish roots, and would constantly rework Spanish subjects. But Spain—even cosmopolitan Barcelona—was simply too provincial for him at the time, and too resistant to change. As Picasso himself later said of an innovative French painter, "If Cézanne had worked in Spain he would have been burnt alive."

Picasso could not then have known of the radical ways in which he was later to change art, but he must have felt that whatever he did, he would be better off in Paris. So in April 1904, he sent his belongings ahead and left Spain. Except for brief visits there, it was for the last time. Having already left his family, he now left his country.

THE BATEAU-LAVOIR

3 UPON ARRIVING IN PARIS, PICASSO MOVED INTO A RUN-DOWN OLD studio and apartment building in Montmartre, which Max Jacob nicknamed the Bateau-Lavoir—the floating laundry—perhaps because it resembled the barges where women did their washing in the Seine, the river that courses through Paris. For many years, this building had been a haven for artists and writers, who lived there together with impoverished actors, clerks, dressmakers, and washerwomen. Picasso would live and work there for the next five years.

It was at the Bateau-Lavoir that Picasso met Fernande Olivier, who became his constant companion and the first important romantic attachment in his life. Six months younger than Picasso, she had left home at the age of seventeen and made, as she put it, "an extremely unhappy try at marriage." She too was living at the Bateau-Lavoir, and one afternoon in a thun-

THE FRUGAL MEAL. *1904. This etching,*
probably reproduced more often than any other by Picasso, again reveals
his sympathy for the poor.

derstorm she ran into Picasso in a corridor of the building. She later wrote in her memoirs, "There was nothing especially attractive about him at first sight. . . . but his radiance, an inner fire one sensed in him, gave him a sort of magnetism, which I was unable to resist." She described him in particular as "small, dark, thickset, restless, disquieting, with gloomy, deep, penetrating eyes, which were curiously still. . . . A thick lock of shiny black hair cut across his intelligent, stubborn forehead. His clothes were half those of a bohemian, half those of a workman, and his long hair brushed the collar of his worn-out coat."

It is from Fernande Olivier's writings that we know most of the details of Picasso's years with her at the Bateau-Lavoir. At first they were always short of money, and they would buy their food on credit from local stores or restaurants. On occasion, they even resorted to trickery: they would order groceries from a shop and have them delivered; when the delivery boy knocked, Fernande would shout through the door, "Put them down, I can't open now; I'm naked!" When he finally gave up and left the parcels, they would open the door and eat, paying for the food when they found the money.

Nor did they enjoy many comforts. There was only one water faucet in the Bateau-Lavoir for all the tenants. In the summer, the building was sweltering. Winters were cold, and their only source of heat was a small coal stove in their room, for which they could not afford the fuel. Olivier remembered spending whole days in bed to stay warm.

When Olivier met Picasso, he was at work on an etching that is perhaps his most famous print: *The Frugal Meal.* Only once, five years before, had Picasso attempted an etching, which is made by scratching a design with a sharp tool into a plate of soft metal such as copper, then filling the lines with ink and pressing paper against the plate to pick up the ink. He was encouraged to make his first print in Barcelona by a friend named Ricardo Canals, who was accomplished at the art. Canals had since moved to Paris and served as Picasso's technical advisor for *The Frugal Meal.*

It is a masterful work and shows how quickly Picasso could learn new techniques—indeed, prints would hereafter play an increasingly important role in his art. *The Frugal Meal* shows a couple seated at a table, with an empty bowl, a bottle of wine, and a small loaf of bread. Their sunken cheeks, thin limbs, and long, bony fingers show that this is not the first time they have suffered a skimpy supper. With its melancholy air and its sympathy for the poor, *The Frugal Meal* is very much in the spirit of the Blue Period.

But late in 1904, Picasso's art went through another metamorphosis. The mood became lighter. Picasso began to work in warmer colors, including

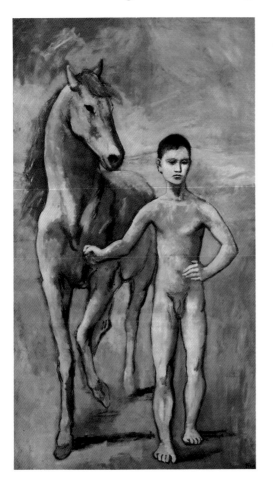

reds, yellows, and a soft rose pink, which has led some people to call this Picasso's Rose Period. Others have called it the Circus Period, because in 1905 he began a series of portraits of clowns, acrobats, and harlequins, all figures from the circus, at which he was a frequent visitor. Unlike the melancholy subjects of the Blue Period, these performers seem to be in control of their lives. Though

BOY LEADING A HORSE.
1906. Another painting from the Rose Period shows the influence on Picasso of his early studies of classical sculptures.

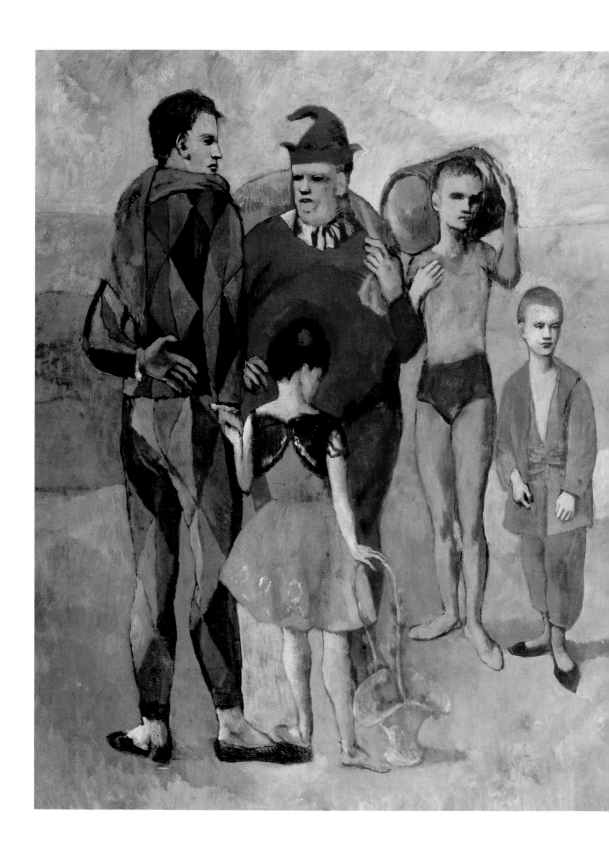

poor and without social status, they are not wedded to despair. It may be that circus figures appealed to Picasso because they were so much like him: they were artists who were impoverished but proud of their talents. Indeed, Picasso sometimes painted the harlequin—the jester who wore a many-colored costume—to resemble himself.

The largest of the circus paintings and the one with the most complex composition is the *Family of Saltimbanques*. It shows several generations of performers, including a portly old man, a young couple, and their children. Saltimbanques are usually thought of as jugglers and tumblers, but here the young man wears the costume of the harlequin and the old man the pointed hat of the buffoon or fool. All the figures are mysteriously quiet, as if awaiting a command. They do not look at each other but beyond each other and out of the painting. Although a family,

■

FAMILY OF SALTIMBANQUES.
1905. This painting of a family of circus acrobats and performers is the most important work of his so-called Rose Period.

they do not seem related, except in the tender way the father holds the hand of his little girl.

It may be that the change in Picasso's painting in 1905 expressed a change in his mood. Slowly, the circumstances of his life were improving. His work attracted the interest of Americans Leo and Gertrude Stein, a brother and sister who were establishing themselves as two of the most perceptive collectors of modern art in Paris at the time. They began to buy his paintings, and Picasso became a frequent visitor at their home. The dealer Vollard, too, continued to buy his work, now at an increased pace.

Moreover, Picasso was surrounded by brilliant and encouraging friends: Max Jacob; the poet and critic Guillaume Apollinaire, who would become one of his principal champions; and the circle of Spanish artists in Paris, who looked to Picasso as a leader. He became a frequent visitor at the cafés of Montparnasse, a district on the left bank of the Seine that was replacing Montmartre as the center of artistic life in Paris. And he was host at frequent get-togethers in his studio. Indeed, so many writers would gather there that one of them suggested Picasso should put a sign over the door: "Au Rendez-vous des Poètes" (meeting place of poets). And he had as a companion a woman who was charming and beautiful.

With all this activity, one might wonder when Picasso had time to work. But through it all, work always came first—he never let distractions, however appealing, interfere with the most important mission in his life. While he had no fixed routine, his afternoons were often devoted to his friends, with whom he would visit in the studio or in the cafés. As a consequence, he would often paint at night, sometimes breaking for another round at the cafés before returning to work. Since he frequently painted until nearly dawn, he would sleep until noon, then get up and start all over again.

In late 1905 and 1906, the character of Picasso's work changed again. His figures became less elongated. They were fuller and rounder, more like the ancient or classical Greek and Roman statues that the artist saw in the Louvre Museum in Paris. Consequently, this is called Picasso's first classical period—first, because Picasso would again paint in a classical manner in the 1920s. An example of this style is the *Boy Leading a Horse,* which conveys a classical mood chiefly through the figure of the boy. Although young, he is muscular, like ancient Greek statues of athletic youths. He and the spirited horse are also idealized in the classical way: they seem almost too perfect to be real. Both are calm and poised but full of energy, like coiled springs. Significantly, no rope connects the boy with his horse. He seems to lead the animal through the force of his character instead.

But Picasso's first classical period was brief. Moreover, it was like the calm before a storm: the artist was on the brink of one of the most shocking metamorphoses of his whole career. In 1907 these quiet, idealized subjects gave way to a ferocious style of painting that even his friends at first found difficult to accept.

LES DEMOISELLES D'AVIGNON

4 PICASSO CONCENTRATED MUCH OF HIS ARTISTIC ENERGY IN 1907 on the creation of a single monumental painting, *Les Demoiselles d'Avignon* (*The Girls of Avignon*). The painting, his largest to that date, shows a group of five nude women posed in front of a blue background. Four are standing, one crouches at the right. The woman at the extreme left holds back a reddish brown drape, as if introducing the other figures.

In its subject matter, the painting recalls many previous works in European painting. Groups of nude female bathers were often portrayed enjoy-

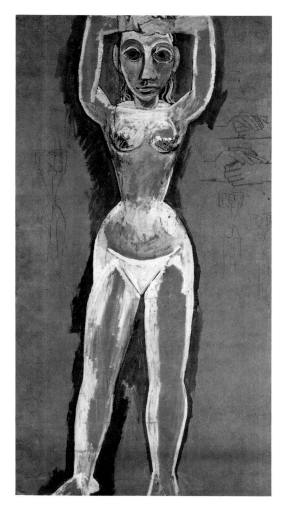

ing themselves in Turkish baths or beside the water out-of-doors. Nudes were also used to suggest moral conflicts: they represented the temptations of the life of the flesh, as opposed to the life of the spirit or of the mind.

Preparatory drawings suggest that Picasso had originally intended this painting as a traditional allegory or representation of moral conflict. It is set in a house of prostitution—the title probably refers to a brothel on Avignon Street in Barcelona. Despite the links the painting may suggest with traditional subject matter, the extraordinary thing about it is the radically untraditional way in which the women are painted. Picasso seems to have wanted to focus our attention not on what he was depicting— the subject—but on how he was depicting it—the style or technique.

To begin with, the figures are flatter than those Picasso had just been painting in his first classical period. Gone are the rounded forms and the naturalistic curves. These women are all angles. Their faces look like masks and are full of distortions: noses are seen in profile, although the faces are presented from the front; eyes are seen from the front, although the rest of the face is in profile.

The two figures at the right are most startling. Their faces are severely elongated, they have tiny mouths and long, flattened ridges that suggest their noses. The left eye of the upper figure is a deep, black hole; those of the lower figure are dislocated, on different levels of the face. Coarse colored stripes, used to suggest shadows, also look like abstract patterns.

The faces of these figures resemble African sculptures, which Picasso was just then discovering for himself at the Trocadéro Museum in Paris, which housed a collection of art from Africa and the Pacific Islands. Al-

STUDY FOR LES DEMOISELLES D'AVIGNON. *1907.*
In his sketch for the painting Picasso was still working out a moral allegory; a sailor represents a life of pleasure among the women and a medical student symbolizes virtue. At left is one of several drawings of single figures that Picasso made.

LES DEMOISELLES D'AVIGNON. *1907.*
A triumph of Picasso's early style combines all his sources of inspiration
and his tremendous creative energy. (Detail at right.)

though such objects had been known in Europe for quite some time, they now became of interest to avant-garde artists, including Picasso. Picasso recognized in the simplification, abstraction, and distortion of form in African and Oceanic sculpture something like what he was trying to achieve.

But Picasso was interested not only in the way these sculptures looked but also in the magical properties he saw in them. They seemed to have the power to speak directly to the imagination, especially to its darker side of horror and fright. "For me the masks were not just sculptures," Picasso later told the writer André Malraux. "They were weapons—to keep people from being ruled by spirits, to help free themselves."

It is this darkly magical quality that Picasso seems to have been striving for in *Les Demoiselles d'Avignon*. With the two figures at the right especially, we realize that Picasso was conveying in stylistic ways powerful feelings of conflict. *Les Demoiselles d'Avignon* suggests complex and contradictory emotions about women. With its combination of seductive and disfigured bodies, the painting suggests that women are both appealing and horrifying, something to be both desired and feared.

Whatever the precise meaning of this painting, it was greeted with confusion even by some of Picasso's admirers. Nearly a century later, it is still a disturbing vision of women, and one many people may find offensive. We can only imagine the full impact it must have had on Picasso's contemporaries. The artists Henri Matisse and Georges Braque, with whom he had recently become friends, were disapproving. Matisse thought it was a hoax, intended to ridicule modern art. Braque said, "It is as though we are supposed to exchange our usual diet for one of tow and paraffin," meaning that the pleasant taste had gone out of Picasso's art; now it was

like eating coarse hemp and wax. Some feared that all this disapproval would lead Picasso to despair. The painter André Derain remarked, "One day we shall find Pablo has hanged himself behind his great canvas."

Even Apollinaire, past and future champion of Picasso's work, was taken aback. He had written in 1905 that "the delightful and the horrible, the low and the delicate, are proportionately mingled" in Picasso's art. Still, he was not entirely prepared for the combination of delight and horror in *Les Demoiselles d'Avignon.* But he would soon come to terms with Picasso's artistic changes and write in 1913, "Never has there been so fantastic a spectacle as the metamorphosis he underwent."

For many years, the painting itself virtually disappeared. It lay forgotten in Picasso's studio and was only exhibited twice in the next thirty years, in 1916 and 1937. Yet none of this deterred Picasso. During the rest of 1907 and into 1908, he worked on a variety of paintings related in spirit both to *Les Demoiselles d'Avignon* and to African sculpture. Perhaps mindful of the shock that *Les Demoiselles* had caused, however, not all were so frightful. The painting *Three Women,* for example, is composed with the same angularity and distortion in the figures as *Les Demoiselles.* But these women are at peace. They are related to their sisters of Avignon, and are every bit as monumental, but they convey an opposite feeling.

In his appreciation of African art, Picasso had shown his ability to recognize expressive power and beauty in things that others found ugly or primitive. In the same way, he came to admire at this time the work of a self-taught painter in Paris named Henri Rousseau. This admiration led Picasso into a curious friendship. Rousseau couldn't

■

THREE WOMEN. *(Detail). 1907. In a work of the same period as* Les Demoiselles *Picasso fractures the female form in geometric, cubist shapes.*

have been less like Picasso: he was a humble and elderly man, a retired employee of the city tax office—naive, whereas Picasso was sophisticated. Yet as artists, Picasso must have felt they shared something important. Rousseau painted fantastical jungle scenes and sleeping gypsies in an almost childlike fashion, with very simple, flat forms. Picasso must have recognized in him another fugitive from academic tradition.

A photograph of Picasso taken about 1910

In 1907 Picasso purchased from a junk shop a full-length portrait of a woman by Rousseau. It became one of his treasured possessions. To honor its creator, Picasso organized in November 1908 one of the most celebrated banquets ever given for an artist. He invited to his studio at the Bateau-Lavoir some thirty of his friends, including Apollinaire, Max Jacob, Braque, and Leo and Gertrude Stein. The studio was decorated, tables set, and a throne put up as a place of honor for Rousseau.

All was well until it was realized that Picasso had ordered the food from the caterer for the following day. Fernande Olivier quickly went to work and prepared a dinner of sardines and rice, but not quickly enough to prevent some of the guests from having too much to drink on empty stomachs. Among those who suffered as a consequence was the painter Marie Laurencin, who must have been unused to alcohol. She stumbled face first into a tray of jam tarts and finally had to be sent home in a taxi.

Through all the confusion, Rousseau slept. He too had had too much to drink, and rested peacefully on his throne. He was not even disturbed by the wax that fell on him from a hanging lantern. As Olivier recounted in her memoirs, "The wax droppings accumulated . . . like a clown's hat on his head, which stayed there until the lantern eventually caught fire. It didn't take much to persuade Rousseau that this was his apotheosis. Then Rousseau, who had brought his violin, started to play a little tune." A more sophisticated artist might have realized that his friends were poking a little fun at him. Yet they sincerely admired his work. Like Picasso's, it was a product of the imagination and not just a copy of the visible world.

By the time of the Rousseau banquet, Picasso was in the midst of yet another artistic metamorphosis. Having left behind the style of *Les Demoiselles d'Avignon,* he embarked, with Braque, on a series of discoveries that would lead to the radically different style known as cubism. With cubism, Picasso and Braque would change the course of modern painting.

THE CUBIST YEARS

5 WITH HINDSIGHT, WE CAN NOW SEE CUBISM FOR WHAT IT WAS: THE most radical transformation of art since the Renaissance. In the fifteenth and sixteenth centuries, Renaissance artists learned to create the illusion of infinite space in their paintings. They developed the system of linear perspective, whereby objects were shown in three dimensions in a space that receded to a distant horizon. Things that were meant to be perceived as close to the viewer were made larger; those that were supposed to be farther away were made smaller. At the same time, artists learned to show the human figure in three dimensions, to make it appear round through the use of light and shadow.

Picasso could paint like a Renaissance master. He could use perspective to

THE RESERVOIR AT HORTA DE EBRO. *1909.*
A landscape of a Spanish hilltop village was one of Picasso's first important
cubist compositions.

create a sense of space and he could paint the human figure in the round. Yet now he chose not to. He developed instead a style that eliminated the illusion of space and turned painting into a composition of geometric shapes on a flat surface. At the same time, he chose not to represent things realistically. Instead, he broke objects apart, representing them in dense networks of fragmented lines and planes. This new style would come to be known as cubism. It would take Picasso closer to abstract art than he had ever gone before and closer than he would ever go again.

Picasso was not alone in his pursuit of this new style. He was accompanied, even guided at times, by his friend Georges Braque. They could not have known how completely they would transform art: they were on an adventure together, unaware of where it would lead. Years later, Picasso recalled, "Almost every evening either I went to Braque's studio or Braque came to mine. Each of us *had* to see what the other had done during the day."

Picasso's statement tells us not only of the closeness of his collaboration with Braque. It tells us also that Picasso was now living more like other people: working in the day, and seeing friends in the evening. But because he often stayed out late at night, he still slept long into the morning. This was a habit he kept throughout most of his life.

Picasso spent the summer of 1909 at Horta in Spain, where he had stayed with his friend Pallarés eleven years before. The austere, rocky landscape and blocky buildings of Horta fitted perfectly with Picasso's newly developing interest in the geometries of nature, and several of his first important cubist works were made there.

One of them, *The Reservoir at Horta de Ebro,* shows how Picasso was taking apart the forms of nature and architecture, breaking them into sharply divided planes of light and dark. These he reassembled on the canvas with a logic that no longer derives from looking at the surface of nature but suggests a crystal or a cut diamond, with surfaces meeting at sharp angles. There is no horizon line or system of perspective in this painting to suggest deep space. Instead, the shapes spread in a pulsating pattern right across the surface of the painting, emphasizing its flatness. The colors are neutral—browns and grays—and take second place to the geometries of the composition.

Back in Paris in the autumn, Picasso continued to refine this new style, and to apply it to other media as well. His *Head of a Woman* (*Fernande*) shows the application of cubist ideas to sculpture, especially in the way

■

STILL LIFE WITH CHAIR CANING. *1912. With his friend Georges Braque, Picasso virtually invented collage, the art of combining different elements, sometimes real objects, with painting and pasted papers.*

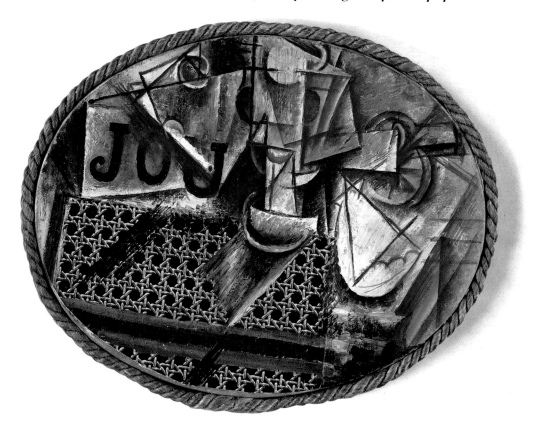

PORTRAIT OF DANIEL-HENRY KAHNWEILER. *1910.*
Called a portrait, this is far from a likeness of its subject, although those who knew him would surely recognize certain characteristics.

HEAD OF A WOMAN. *1909. Picasso applied cubist geometry to sculpture in a portrait of his mistress, Fernande Olivier.*

■

the face is broken into separate planes that meet at sharp angles. But in this sculpture, as in the painting *The Reservoir at Horta de Ebro*, the subject is still recognizable. Over the course of the next year, this would become less and less true of Picasso's art.

The *Portrait of Daniel-Henry Kahnweiler*, painted in the autumn of 1910, shows how far Picasso would go in disintegrating form. Kahnweiler, who had become Picasso's dealer and who was the champion and historian of cubism, is hardly recognizable here. The entire canvas is covered with tiny geometric shapes, which read more as an abstract pattern than as a portrait. Only gradually do the features of the sitter emerge—the plane of the nose, the curve of the mouth, the fingers of the crossed hands. So rigorously did Picasso dissect his figures then that Apollinaire would later write of him "assassinating" anatomy "with the science and technique of a great surgeon."

However abstract this painting looks, Picasso would never abandon representation altogether. He always started from nature, whether it was a figure, a landscape, or a still life. "There is no abstract art," Picasso claimed many years later. "You must always start with something. Afterward you can remove all traces of reality." The challenge for Picasso seemed to be to transform these subjects as much as he could without letting go of them entirely, so that we can feel a tension between their natural shapes and the forms they took in the artist's imagination. Cubist reality, he would later assert, is "not a reality you can take in your hand. It's more like a perfume. . . . The scent [of reality] is everywhere but you don't quite know where it comes from."

Despite the difficulty of these works, Picasso continued to be successful. He had the unwavering support of Kahnweiler, and collectors continued to buy his work. By the autumn of 1909, he was able to move to the Boulevard de Clichy and larger quarters, which included both a vast studio and an adjoining apartment. No longer would he live in the colorful but cramped spaces of the Bateau-Lavoir, although he would keep his studio there until 1912.

Fernande Olivier remembered this move with mixed feelings. Suddenly, they were living in a large apartment with a maid to wait on them. But she felt less and less a part of Picasso's life. "Loyal companion during the years of hardship," she wrote, "I was not to share the prosperous years ahead." Indeed, by the autumn of 1911, Picasso had found a new love and a new inspiration for his art: Eva Gouel Humbert, whom he called Ma Jolie (My Pretty), after the name of a popular song. This name would appear on a number of his most important cubist works.

■

GUITAR. *1912–13. Scraps of wood, cardboard, paper, a tin can, and some wire make up this whimsical musical instrument.*

The years 1911 and 1912 mark a watershed in the history of cubism. Braque and Picasso worked very closely in those years, spending time together not only in Paris but also during the summer in the south of France. Both started to expand the vocabulary of cubism. They began by adding words and numbers to their works. Then they started to experiment with collage, incorporating actual pieces of newspaper, sheet music, wallpaper, and other materials into paintings. Rather than breaking objects apart as they did in their earlier cubist compositions, they now began to build them up with cut-out shapes. Bottles, guitars, fruit, and faces were playfully put together from scraps of pasted paper.

Picasso's first collage was *Still Life with Chair Caning.* Like many of the cubist collages, this one takes its subject from the café. A dissected pipe, a goblet, a lemon, and a few letters from the title of a newspaper are painted around and on top of a piece of oilcloth that carries the printed pattern of a chair seat. This is not real chair caning: Picasso used it because it tricks you into thinking it is real, until you look closely and see that it is not. Around it all, a piece of mariner's rope is wrapped, which parodies the fancy gold-leaf frames found on old-master paintings. One has the sense that Picasso was having fun making this collage, combining materials that had little to do with each other, and that had not before been used in art.

Collage made many things possible. It could be used to make three-dimensional "picture reliefs," as well as full-blown sculptures. Braque made a number of cut-out sculptures in 1911, and Picasso quickly followed suit. These too were radically unlike anything seen before. Traditional sculptures of the human figure, for example, have an inside and an outside, a volume and a surface. These sculptures do not: you can look inside of them and see how they are constructed.

Picasso and Braque worked closely in these years; they were also good friends. They sometimes dressed alike in mechanic's overalls to suggest that they felt like inventors, rather than traditional artists. The people they seem to have identified with the most were Wilbur and Orville Wright, American brothers who had just invented the airplane. Picasso sometimes called Braque "Wilbourg" after one of the Wrights, perhaps because Braque's sculptures, now lost, looked like the Wrights' biplane.

But by 1914, the heady days of cubism were over. World War I broke out, and Braque enlisted in the army. In August of that year, Picasso saw him off to the front from the Avignon train station. When Braque returned from the war two years later, he was a changed man. Picasso had changed too. Although he occasionally worked in a cubist style, he moved on to other things. Picasso did run into Braque from time to time, but their friendship was not the same. In any meaningful sense, he never saw Braque again.

THE ESTABLISHED ARTIST

6 THE COMING OF WAR BROUGHT MANY CHANGES TO PICASSO'S LIFE. Braque was only one of his many friends who left Paris. Apollinaire, though not a French citizen, joined the artillery. Kahnweiler, a German national and hence an enemy alien, went into exile in a neutral country. Deepening the gloom caused by the war, Picasso suffered other, more personal, losses at the same time. Max Jacob, who had experienced a vision of Christ some years before, decided he wanted to withdraw into monastic life. Born a Jew, he first had to convert to Christianity. In early 1915 he was baptized, with Picasso as his godfather. Thereafter, Picasso would see less and less of his old friend. Finally, late that year, Picasso's beloved Eva died, after a short and terrible illness.

Not surprisingly, the combination of war and personal crisis coin-

**PORTRAIT OF OLGA IN
AN ARMCHAIR.** *1917. Even after
years of working in a cubist style,
Picasso could return to realistic detail
with ease, here portraying his wife-to-be
shortly after they met.*

cided with a pronounced change in Picasso's work. On the one hand, he continued to produce cubist-inspired paintings such as *Harlequin*, a circus figure, of 1915. Although entirely composed in oil, it looks as if it were constructed out of collaged paper. On the other hand, he began a series of painstakingly realistic pencil portraits of his friends, including Ambroise Vollard, Max Jacob, and Apollinaire. These led ultimately to portraits in oil, including *Olga in an Armchair* of 1917.

Picasso met Olga Koklova, the subject of this portrait, in Rome, where he had gone to work on a production for the Russian Ballet, a cosmopolitan company headed by the impresario Sergei Diaghilev. Although Picasso had always been more interested in the circus and the cabaret than the ballet, he had been persuaded to collaborate with the poet Jean Cocteau and the composer Erik Satie on a production for the company. Perhaps he was convinced by the fact that Cocteau and Satie were, like him, among the most avant-garde artists in France at the time. But no doubt he was also enticed by the subject of the proposed ballet.

Parade, as it was called, was to be a burlesque or parody of the kind of music-hall entertainments that Picasso adored. There would be four dancers—a Chinese magician, a little girl, and two acrobats. Satie's music, "like a village band," would be accompanied by the sounds of an airplane, a siren, and a typewriter. Picasso would paint the drop curtain and add some characters of his own invention to the ballet—three "managers," larger than life-size figures that were completely covered by cubist constructions. Preparations for the ballet were made in Rome in the early spring, and it was given its premiere in Paris in May 1917.

The enormous cubist figures, the strange music, the sight of the little girl riding a bike and buying a camera instead of dancing—all this caused an uproar. The audience felt the production was a joke at their expense. Once again, it was Apollinaire who stepped into the breach. He had written the program notes for the ballet, which he said heralded a new spirit in art. He saw in it a kind of "sur-realism." That is to say, the shocking juxtapositions of sights and sounds were intended to disrupt conventional ways of looking at things and make people see them as if for the first time. This was apparently the first use of the term "surrealism," which would become so important in the 1920s and 1930s, defining the

HARLEQUIN. *1915. Quite different from his early circus figures, this clown is completely cubist.*

spirit of art in those decades.

Picasso spent much of the next several years designing costumes and scenery for other ballet productions for Diaghilev, including *The Three-Cornered Hat* and *Pulcinella,* the latter with music by Igor Stravinsky. Moreover, it was through his attachment to the ballet that Picasso met the woman who would become his first wife—Olga Koklova. She was a dancer in Diaghilev's company, and when the company left Europe for South America after the opening of *Parade,* she remained behind with Picasso. They were married in the summer of 1918 and moved into a well-furnished apartment on the Rue la Boétie in a fashionable neighborhood in the center of Paris.

With Olga, Picasso began a life of comfortable sophistication. The war ended in the autumn of 1918, shortly after they married, and those of their friends who survived the war reassembled in Paris. But life was not to be the same for Picasso—he was drifting away from his prewar friends and the radical nature of his prewar art. Apollinaire came back, but he soon died from influenza, during the epidemic that coincided with the Armistice. Braque came back, but he felt alienated from Picasso's new way of life—his wealthy friends, his fashionable clothes, his ties to the theater. At the same time, Picasso also withdrew from

FAMILY ON THE SEA-SHORE. *(Detail). 1922. Following the birth of his first child, Picasso made several paintings of women and children, showing figures out-of-doors, often nude or wearing robes like togas.*

his earlier, single-minded pursuit of new forms in art. He began to rediscover classical forms and subjects.

In some cases, Picasso's art from the early 1920s was drawn directly from classical myths. For example, he executed line drawings of centaurs, the beasts who were half man and half horse. In other cases, it was the style of the works that gave them their classical feeling. Picasso began painting compositions dominated by colossal nudes, such as *Family on the Seashore* of 1922. Here, the fullness of the figures suggests the roundness and solidity of ancient Greek or Roman sculpture. It may be that Picasso was moved to paint such family scenes by the fact that Olga was then expecting a child— she would bear a son, called Paulo, in early 1921. Picasso followed with a number of paintings of mothers and children.

But while Picasso was thus perfecting his classical style, he was still composing pictures in the flat, geometric forms of cubism. In the summer of 1921, for example, he created two versions of a monumental cubist composition called *Three Musicians.* In both, three larger–than–life-sized figures sit at a table. In the later version, shown here, a monk is seated to the right, his dark robes bound by a rope. On the left is a harlequin in colorful costume playing a violin. Between them is a pierrot, a figure associated with pantomime. He is

■

THREE MUSICIANS. *1921.*

The bold, large painting is one of the last that Picasso made in the cubist style.

dressed in a white costume and plays a clarinet. With their strange masks, these figures are witty, but also a little sinister. They could not be more different from the serene, full-bodied figures of *Family on the Seashore.*

No matter how different they may be, however, *Three Musicians* and *Family on the Seashore* are alike in one respect. Picasso would not make many more paintings like them, in either his cubist or his classical style. He may have wanted to bring this phase of his artistic life to a close, in anticipation of yet another radical change of direction.

Once again, it is tempting to find a parallel to this artistic restlessness in Picasso's personal life. In these years, Picasso appeared to be settled for good. He at last had a wife and a child, a comfortable home, and a respectability so different from the bohemian life of his youth. Yet it was not to last. Picasso must have felt a conflict between the man he had been and the man he had become. The same restlessness that would propel changes in his art would soon tear apart his home.

THE SURREALIST YEARS

7 IN 1925 PICASSO PAINTED A LARGE CANVAS CALLED *THREE DANCERS.* Three nude women, their hands joined, dance in a circle. But these figures are not depicted with the full-bodied forms of Picasso's classical period or the logically constructed geometries of cubism. They are radically, even violently, distorted, with long thin limbs, sharp angles, and dislocated features. The same year, Picasso painted *The Kiss,* in which the lovers seem ready to devour each other. Their faces especially are distorted, almost beyond recognition. Both paintings project a kind of desperate ecstasy. There had been nothing like them in Picasso's art since *Les Demoiselles d'Avignon.*

By this time, Picasso had met André Breton and others of the new group of surrealist artists in Paris. Breton had published his *Manifesto of Surrealism* in 1924, in which the ideas of the group were given their first expression. The group aimed to explore the sources of creativity, especially those in the subconscious mind. Building on the teachings of the psychologist Sigmund Freud, they wanted to reveal the part that dreams, visions, and irrational impulses could play in making art. They would create in a kind of "dream state." If this led them into forbidden territory, into the realm of nightmares and of violence, so much the better. Beauty, Breton wrote, had to be "convulsive." It should make the observer shudder, or give a sensation of fright, as it connects with repressed feelings in the subconscious.

Although he maintained a distance from them, Picasso both supported and was supported by the surrealists. They recognized in *Les Demoiselles d'Avignon* a forerunner of their ideas. In 1924, Breton was instrumental in persuading a private collector to purchase the painting from Picasso.

It was perhaps because of his contact with the surrealists that Picasso returned to painting the kind of ferocious images that he had begun exploring nearly twenty years before but virtually abandoned since then. *Three Dancers* is but the first of many works in these years that tear apart the female figure and reconstruct it as if in a nightmare. The *Seated Woman* of 1927, for example, seems both frightened and frightening. Her pale face is set against a hood of hair that rises like a serpent from her body. She stares out in horror, while a disk-eyed shadow returns the gaze. There is a feeling of foreboding, of anxiety, in this painting, as if Picasso were anticipating the horrors that would descend on Europe in the course of the next decade. Ultimately, the monstrous aspects of human nature revealed by the Spanish Civil War and World War II would find explicit expression in Picasso's art.

Meanwhile, Picasso's personal life began to show signs of stress. As the years passed, he grew more and more distant from Olga. He felt trapped by the responsibilities of family and began to rebel against the ordered and fashionable life they led. Years later he would say of Olga, "She asked too much of me." Picasso evidently continued to feel a conflict between his domestic responsibilities and his work; he also seems to have craved more

personal freedom, whatever the consequences to his family. Although it would still be many years before he made the final break with Olga, it was clear their relationship was deteriorating by 1927. That year, Picasso met on the street in Paris a young, athletic-looking woman named Marie-Thérèse Walter, who replaced Olga as the focus of his affections. She was seventeen; he was forty-five.

The disquiet in Picasso's life during these years found expression not only in the figures of women, but in other subjects as well. In 1930, for example, Picasso tackled a subject that for him was highly unusual. He painted *The Crucifixion,*

THE KISS. *1925. At the time Picasso painted this unsettling work, he was meeting with artists who believed in using dreams, nightmares, and other visions in their creations.*

one of the few overtly religious subjects he ever treated. Parts of the painting come directly from the story of Christ's death: the figure nailing Christ's hand to the cross, the soldier on horseback, and the bodies of the two thieves lying on the ground at the bottom left. Prominent in the

SEATED WOMAN. *1927.*

Flattening the figure out so that two sides are seen at once lends an air of mystery and fright to this "portrait."

center of the composition is the figure of the wailing Mary Magdalene, her face contorted, her mouth open and her teeth exposed like so many of Picasso's women of these years.

But other parts of *The Crucifixion* seem to come from Picasso's imagination. What, for example, is the large, green, rocklike shape that floats to the left of the cross? It may be, as one writer has suggested, the sponge soaked with vinegar that Christ was offered when he called for water, but enlarged to monstrous proportions. And what of the strange, hooded, yellow figure to the right, or the disembodied pair of arms next to it? The one seems threatening, the other pleading. By combining conventional elements of the Crucifixion with these figures from his own imagination, Picasso seems to have been trying to make this painting both a narrative of Christ's death and a universal symbol of brutality and suffering.

In 1931 Picasso bought a small, seventeenth-century château in the countryside outside of Paris, at the edge of a small village called Boisgeloup. Unlike his apartment in Paris, this château with its outbuildings gave him ample room, and he turned again to making sculpture, some of it at a very large scale. That summer, he executed a number of monumental heads of women with the face of Marie-Thérèse Walter. In the bronze *Bust of a Woman,* for example, the features are quite regular except for the nose, which emerges uninterrupted from the hair and forehead. Even with this distortion, the face is noble and serene. Despite the violence of much of Picasso's work of these years, there remains this tender side, perhaps inspired by affection for Marie-Thérèse. She would be an important part of Picasso's life for several more years: together they would have a daughter named Maria Concepción, or Maia, in 1935, the year of his final break from Olga.

Picasso's reputation as an artist continued to grow in these years. He was given exhibitions in New York and London as well as in Paris. The most important was his first retrospective, in which 225 paintings spanning his whole career were shown together with sculptures and illustrated books. The exhibition was held at the Galerie Georges Petit, Paris, in June and July 1932. That autumn, it was shown at the Kunsthaus, Zurich, one of the leading museums in Switzerland. Meanwhile, the art magazine *Cahiers d'art* devoted a special issue to Picasso, and when his exhibition opened in Zurich, he was the subject of an article by the noted psychologist Carl Jung.

Picasso spent part of the summer of 1933 in Barcelona, where he renewed his interest in the bullfight. Back in Boisgeloup in September, he painted a number of pictures based on the combat. *Bullfight: Death of the Torero* shows the bull victorious, with the bullfighter impaled on his horns and

■

THE CRUCIFIXION.
1930. A subject of artists for centuries, Christ's death on the cross has seldom been pictured with such violence.

the red cloak trampled under his feet. The torero's horse turns in terror and in pain: he has been gored in the stomach, and his intestines hang out.

Two years later, Picasso made an extraordinary print, *Minotauromachia,* which is related to the bullfight pictures. But here, the animal has been transformed into a Minotaur. This legendary beast, half man and half bull, made his first appearance in Picasso's art in these years. He is a figure both of power and of terror—this was the creature to which young men and women were sacrificed. Here, too, the beast is victorious. The bullfighter, a woman this time, lies dead across the back of her horse, which has again been wounded in the stomach. At the far left, a man climbs a ladder, as if to escape. Only a young girl, holding a candle and a bouquet of flowers, stands her ground. The Minotaur advances toward her, but whether she will tame the beast or be devoured by him remains a mystery. This is a strange and powerful print, rich in Picasso's private symbolism.

Whatever its precise meaning, the conflict between man and beast represented here and in the bullfight pictures would continue to be of great importance in Picasso's art through the second half of the decade. Although Picasso was no doubt interested in the drama of the fight between man and animal for its own sake, he would also use it to suggest the combat between good and evil, as in *Minotauromachia.* The bullfight would figure again in one of the most important paintings Picasso ever made, *Guernica.*

■

BUST OF A WOMAN. *1931. Picasso made several monumental heads in the 1930s using Marie-Thérèse Walter as a model.*

64

GUERNICA: PICASSO AT WAR

8 ON APRIL 26, 1937, NAZI GERMAN BOMBERS FLYING UNDER ORDERS from General Francisco Franco laid waste the town of Guernica, in the Basque part of Spain, killing many innocent civilians. Franco, the Fascist leader who was in league with Adolf Hitler, had the previous year begun his rebellion against the legally elected Republican government of Spain, thereby beginning the Spanish Civil War. Picasso, Spanish-born and a supporter of the government, was quickly drawn into the conflict. He sold his work to raise money for the Republican cause and accepted the government's request that he become director of the Prado, the most important museum in Spain. In the midst of the war, the government asked Picasso to create a large mural to hang in the Spanish pavilion at the Exposition Universelle (World's Fair) in Paris in 1937. The bombing of Guernica, a town loyal to the government, provided Picasso with a subject.

Guernica bears witness to Picasso's horror and outrage. Throughout the huge composition—it is nearly twenty-six feet wide—can be seen victims of the catastrophe: a woman falling from a burning building; a crying woman holding her dead baby in her arms; a dead soldier, his body in fragments. But in Picasso's typical way, *Guernica* does not give a factual report of the bombing but uses distortion to convey an emotionally powerful image of destruction. At its heart are the symbolic images of horse and bull, the familiar adversaries of the bullfight paintings. While the horse is clearly a victim of the attack, the bull is more difficult to interpret. He is not himself responsible for the destruction but stands as an emblem of the powerful, terrible forces that caused it. Picasso later confirmed this reading of the painting when he said to an American soldier,

BULL'S HEAD. *1942.*
Picasso assembled this sculpture
from the seat and handlebars
of a bicycle, probably found
abandoned on the street.

"The bull . . . is brutality and darkness. . . . The horse represents the people."

To paint *Guernica,* Picasso had taken a new and larger studio on the Rue des Grands-Augustins in Paris. Gradually, Picasso abandoned the studio and apartment on the Rue de la Boétie (where he had lived since the end of World War I) as well as the château at Boisgeloup, all of which he had shared with Olga. For a time, he lived with Marie-Thérèse and Maia in a small house outside of Paris, but soon a new infatuation caused him to separate from this family as well. Through the surrealist artists, Picasso had met in 1936 a young painter and photographer named Dora Maar. Maar now took over the role of helper and muse, or inspiration. She was instrumental in finding the space where Picasso created *Guernica* and took a series of photographs that documented the painting over several weeks.

Picasso's work in these years continued to range between explorations of violence and cruelty and paintings of a more light-hearted kind. He painted still lifes, for example, and affectionate portraits of Marie-Thérèse and Maia. He also made portraits of Dora Maar. One, dated 1937, shows her seated in an armchair, with one hand held to her cheek. There are jarring elements to this painting. Maar's skin is painted a brilliant yellow and her face is distorted—she is shown in profile, but with both eyes on the same side of her nose. Nevertheless, this is a quiet, dignified portrait, showing Picasso's awareness of both the beauty and the intelligence of the subject.

Picasso passed a major professional milestone in these years as well. Late in 1939, he was given his largest retrospective to date, at the Museum of Modern Art in New York. Called "Picasso: Forty Years of His Art," the exhibition included more than three hundred works, many already in the museum's collection, such as *Les Demoiselles d'Avignon.* It also included *Guernica,* which had been shown to great acclaim in London, Chicago, Los Angeles, and San Francisco. Picasso continued to be prosperous, and to spend his summers in the south of France.

But Picasso would soon be caught up in events that were larger than he was. In 1939 World War II began. In the spring of 1940, the German army swept through Holland and Belgium into France, and occupied Paris. Picasso's adopted home was now under the control of the people he hated most: the Fascists who had aided Franco in the destruction of Guernica. Picasso was urged to take refuge in Mexico or the United States, for the Nazis had already denounced him as a "degenerate" modern artist, and people feared for his safety.

But Picasso chose to stay in Paris, and remained there for the duration of

MINOTAUROMACHIA. *1935.*
Like his great Spanish predecessor Francisco Goya,
Picasso made a series of etchings relating to bulls,
but Picasso's work draws ideas, images, and
styles from many more sources.

being celebrated in a town where some people were still under the influence of Nazi propaganda. To make matters more difficult, the day before the exhibition opened it was announced that Picasso had joined the French Communist party. Picasso explained that he did this because he felt the Communists "worked the hardest to understand and construct the world . . . that they had been the bravest" in fighting against the Fascists in France and Spain. Moreover, many of his friends were Communists. But Picasso's alliance with the Communists was never an easy one. He was far too individualistic as a person and as an artist to fit in with their ideas that art must be easy to understand and serve the interests of the party. While he designed posters for them and attended several party congresses, within a few years he began to drift away from the Communists.

During the war years, Picasso's work ranged again between very different styles, as exemplified by two remarkable sculptures he made in 1942 and 1943. One is the *Bull's Head*, assembled from found objects: the leather seat and metal handlebars of a bicycle. Picasso was particularly pleased with this sculpture because it showed how things could be combined and transformed into something else. He was amused by the idea that one

PORTRAIT OF DORA MAAR. *(Detail). 1937. In 1936 Picasso took up with artist Dora Maar.*

the war. The Nazis prohibited him from exhibiting his work publicly, although privately they came to court him. Picasso kept his distance. They offered him food and fuel to warm his studio, which would have made his life more comfortable in those years of shortages. But Picasso refused. "A Spaniard is never cold," he said. Once, a German officer saw a photograph of *Guernica* in his studio. "Did you do this?" the German demanded to know. "No," Picasso answered. "You did." He even distributed postcards of the painting to Germans who came to see him. Picasso left no doubt as to which side he was on and whom he held responsible for the horror of the war.

Picasso never joined the Resistance, which struggled undercover against the Nazi occupation. But his presence in Paris during the war and his refusal to cooperate with the Germans made him a symbol of freedom, of the unvanquished spirit, during the dark years of the occupation. In fact, when the war ended and the Paris art world celebrated liberation with a special show in the autumn of 1944, Picasso was given a gallery to himself.

Not everyone was pleased. Two days after the exhibition opened, a demonstration took place in the Picasso gallery and several of his paintings were ripped down from the walls. Here was a Spaniard being honored in an important French exhibition, and a "degenerate" modern artist

GUERNICA. *1937.*

*This painting, made in Paris during Spain's
civil war and loaned to the Museum of Modern
Art in New York until long after World War II,
was finally given to the people of Spain
when Picasso was assured that his country
would be governed by the people themselves
and not by a dictator.*

DEATH'S HEAD. *1943.*

*The war in Europe was in its darkest
hours when Picasso made this powerful sculpture,
so different in mood from the* Bull's Head
made only the year before.

**BULLFIGHT:
DEATH OF THE
TORERO.** *(Detail). 1933.
As a Spaniard, it is not
surprising that Picasso was
fascinated all his life
with the bullfight.*

■

day they might be transformed back again. He said, "Out of the handlebars and the bicycle seat I made a bull's head which everybody recognized as a bull's head. Thus a metamorphosis was completed; and now I would like to see another metamorphosis take place in the opposite direction. Suppose my bull's head is thrown on the scrap heap. Perhaps some day a fellow will come along and say: 'Why, there's something that would come in very handy for the handlebars of my bicycle.'"

The darker side of Picasso's work during the war is shown in the other sculpture, the bronze *Death's Head*. It is one of the simplest sculptures Picasso ever made, and one of the most expressive. The eyes are nothing but dark, hollow circles; the mouth is a jagged cut. The surface is smooth, like polished bone. Picasso knew that death was all around him during the war. In early 1944, his old friend Max Jacob, who had become a Catholic and was living in a monastery, was arrested by the Nazis because he had been born a Jew. He was sent to a concentration camp and died very soon thereafter. Despite the risk, Picasso attended his funeral in Paris.

When liberation came, Picasso's sense of relief and happiness also found expression in his art. As allied troops approached Paris to drive out the Nazis, and fighting erupted in the streets of the city, Picasso began work on a scene of frantic joy, the *Bacchanale after Poussin*. Based on a painting done by the French artist Nicolas Poussin in 1638–39, Picasso's *Bacchanale* (now unfortunately lost) was nevertheless entirely his own. It showed a group of revelers celebrating Bacchus, the ancient Greek god of wine and fertility. In a forest glen, naked figures danced in a circle while a trumpet sounded and goats ran through the crowd. Their ecstasy was shown by the elongation of arms and legs and the wild distortion of bodies and heads. Over it all presided the figure of Pan, god of pastures and animal herds. This was a painting that shouted, for Picasso and for France, "The war is over!"

THE INTERNATIONAL CELEBRITY

9 THE EXPERIENCE OF WAR DID NOT INSTANTLY DROP OUT OF PI-
casso's mind. In the summer of 1945, he made a painting called
The Charnel House, which recalled *Guernica* in its violence
and its anger about the war. It was painted at the time that the
world was beginning to understand the full horror of the concentration
camps, of the murder of millions of Jews and other people that the Nazis had
persecuted. It shows a pile of tied and mangled bodies, portrayed only in the
most somber colors of black and white. Unlike *Guernica,* where the rushing
figures scream, these bodies are still and silent. They are Picasso's memorial to the victims of the Nazi terror.

At the same time, the happiness of the little *Bacchanale after Poussin*
found expression in a far larger work, *La Joie de Vivre (The Joy of Life),* of
1946. Picasso spent that summer in Antibes, on the Mediterranean coast of
France, for the first time since the war began. He met the curator of the
Antibes Museum, located in the old Grimaldi castle high above the port, who
offered to let him work in one of the museum's big, empty rooms. There
Picasso took up a number of Mediterranean themes, such as still lifes with
fish and sea urchins, fishermen, and mythological subjects. *La Joie de
Vivre* was one of these.

Picasso was not only celebrating the end of war in this painting.
He also had more personal happiness to express. During the
war, he had met a young painter named Françoise Gilot, who
had become his constant companion by this time. Soon they

■

*Picasso with his second wife, Jacqueline,
whom he married in 1961, and a visitor to his studio*

78

would have a child together, a boy named Claude, who was born in the spring of 1947. Two years later, Françoise gave birth to a girl, whom they named Paloma, the Spanish word for dove. Françoise and their new children became frequent subjects for Picasso in these years.

Among the images he made of them is the painting *Claude Drawing, Françoise and Paloma,* of 1954, which suggests complete contentment and tranquillity. Again, however, it would not last for long.

Picasso and Françoise spent most of these years with their new family in the south of France, living in a small town named Vallauris. Picasso had become interested in making ceramics, and the town had been known for its pottery for hundreds of years. Working with local craftsmen, Picasso took on this new medium with great enthusiasm. He also devoted a great deal of creative energy to sculpture in these years, with inventive results. He playfully combined a variety of found objects, just as he had with the *Bull's Head* during the war, and metamorphosed them into completely different things.

Baboon and Young, for example, is made from discarded pottery, metal, plaster, and two model cars, which give the animal its face. These machine forms are easily made by Picasso to look like organic shapes they were never meant to resemble. While Picasso is making an obvious joke with this sculpture, it is much more than that. He is also creating a modern monster like a Minotaur, with the head of a machine and the body of an animal. It is this suggestion of myth that makes the sculpture so fascinating.

By now, Picasso was over seventy years old. Yet he was living the life of a much

BABOON AND YOUNG.
1951. The head of this fantastical creature is cast from a toy car.

THE CHARNEL HOUSE. *1945. Picasso created a memorial to the victims of Nazi concentration camps.*

■

younger man, with infant children, and with creative energies that were as strong as ever. Occasionally, however, he began to look back over his life and his long career. Although he had sometimes made paintings before that recalled the work of earlier artists — *Bacchanale after Poussin,* for example — he now undertook a whole series of such paintings. He did free variations on compositions by the Eugène Delacroix and Diego Velázquez. It was as if he wanted to measure himself against the old masters, to see if, after a lifetime of work, he could claim to be as good as they were.

Women of Algiers, shown on pages 86–87, was the last of some fifteen variations that Picasso made on the Delacroix original, a scene of North African women seated quietly in a harem. Picasso's treatment of the subject is dominated by the figure of a woman in a Moorish headdress. Her body is full and rounded, almost like a statue. On the rug beside her another woman reclines. She is all angles and flat planes, almost the opposite of the first woman. Picasso sets up a vivid contrast between these women, as he did years earlier in *Les Demoiselles d'Avignon.* Yet here, the menacing quality is gone. These women of Algiers are all vigorous and appealing.

This cheerful vision of women coincided with the beginning of Picasso's relationship with Jacqueline Roque, which would last for the rest of his life. For some time, Picasso and Françoise Gilot had been experiencing difficulties. He was never comfortable with having a full-time family. For her part, Gilot felt that her own needs as a person and ambitions as an artist were always second to Picasso's—that she lived to help him and not enough for herself. In the autumn of 1953, she left him and moved back to Paris. It was not long after that Picasso's relationship with Jacqueline Roque became serious. They left the house in Vallauris, where he had lived with Gilot, and settled together in 1955 in a large, ornate villa called La Californie in the hills above Cannes. Picasso continued to see his children in the summer and at holidays, but after his move to Cannes, he never saw Gilot again.

Picasso's years with Jacqueline, whom he married in 1961, mark the final phase of his life. These were years in which Picasso achieved worldwide recognition—few artists have achieved such fame in their lifetime. He was honored with more and more exhibitions, which were seen by millions of people. Picasso's fame also resulted in many invitations to adorn public spaces and buildings with his art. In 1957, for example, he agreed to create an enormous mural for a United Nations building in Paris, the headquarters of the Educational, Scientific, and Cultural Organization (UNESCO). And in

1963 he was invited to create a monumental sculpture for the new civic center in downtown Chicago.

Picasso was not always happy with the attention he received. He found the life of a celebrity very wearing, with people always wanting to see him. He felt spied upon by the crowds that gathered outside of his house. In 1960 he told the photographer Brassaï, "I live in seclusion, like a prisoner. I would not wish my celebrity on anyone, not even my worst enemies. I suffer from it, physically. I protect myself as best I can. I barricade myself behind doors that are kept double-locked night and day."

To make matters worse for Picasso, Cannes was growing rapidly. Tall apartment buildings that looked down into his garden were being built around his home. In an effort to secure more privacy, Picasso in 1958 bought an enormous, fourteenth-century château some fifty miles inland, at Vauvenargues, on the slope of Monte Sainte-Victoire, in a landscape made famous by Cézanne.

■

CHICAGO MONUMENT. *1964.*
In his mid-eighties Picasso still tackled new challenges, such as this huge metal sculpture, larger by far than anything he had ever done.

Made of heavy masonry with round towers at the corners and set in a wild pine forest, the château provided Picasso with a refuge from the crowds and the frivolity of Cannes, as well as a vast space for his work.

In a few years, however, the spell of Vauvenargues weakened. Picasso began looking for a place to live closer to Cannes and the sea. In 1961 he

LA JOIE DE VIVRE (THE JOY OF LIFE). *1946.*
Here, Picasso celebrates the end of the war and a new love in his life.

■

(Following pages) **WOMEN OF ALGIERS** *(After Delacroix). 1955.*
To link himself with great past artists, Picasso made variations of their works.

found a villa on top of a hill near Mougins, just five miles from Cannes. Called Le Mas Notre-Dame-de-Vie, the villa was private, spacious, and had excellent views of the sea and the mountains. It became his final home.

Picasso's last years were as productive as any in his long life. He made dozens of portraits of his young wife and in paintings and engravings

repeatedly took up the theme of the artist and his model. He returned with great enthusiasm to subjects from earlier years, such as the circus, the bullfight, and the theater. In one extraordinary summer, 1968, he produced as many as 347 engravings. His production of paintings was no less phenomenal, with many on the theme of love and the family. For the first time in many years, he began making self-portraits as well. In some of them, the face begins to look like a death mask, with protruding eyes. Although his energy seldom gave out, there is no doubt that Picasso was beginning to feel his own mortality.

But the tone of his late work is surprisingly vigorous, even optimistic. Much of it seems autobiographical. When he depicted the artist and his model, for example, or scenes of love, he was looking back on the things that had truly mattered to him in his life. Even works that were not obviously autobiographical had a retrospective element. In painting *The Matador*, for example, Picasso was not only reminding us of his admiration for these performers. He was also expressing the way he, as another kind of artist, identified with their independence,

THE MATADOR. *1970.*

This is one of Picasso's last treatments of a favorite subject.

their courage, and their skill. These were the very qualities that had made Picasso the individual artist that he was, even into his old age.

Picasso died at Le Mas Notre-Dame-de-Vie on April 8, 1973, at the age of ninety-one. He was buried two days later in the garden of the château at Vauvenargues. Only Jacqueline, his son Paulo, and a few friends were present. His family conflicts followed him to the grave. Claude and Paloma were not invited to the funeral—they had become estranged from their father, particularly since 1964, when their mother published memoirs of her stormy relationship with Picasso. Matters were made even more difficult in 1969 when a lawsuit was filed on their behalf, to insure that they would inherit from him even though their parents had never married. This conflict was not resolved until after Picasso's death, when the French government made them, and his other illegitimate child, Maia, legal heirs.

During his life, Picasso kept an enormous quantity of his own work. After his death, the French government allowed a portion of this treasure to be given to the French people in place of inheritance taxes. It now forms the nucleus of the Picasso Museum in Paris, which opened in 1985. This instantly became the largest collection of Picasso's art, but not the only one, for his works are also found in numerous other museums around the world.

Thus was Picasso's rich legacy preserved for the public. Future generations will always be able to see the extraordinary accomplishments of this magical man, who dominated the art of his century. He will always be celebrated, for he painted for the heart and the soul no less than for the eye and the mind. As much as any other artist before or since, he laid bare the exhilarating heights and the horrible depths of human life, from the pleasures of love to the terrors of modern warfare. He was the artist who above all others in this century gave visible form to our nightmares and our visions. He materialized his dreams, and ours.

LIST OF ILLUSTRATIONS

Oil and oilcloth on canvas edged with rope, $11\frac{3}{8} \times 14\frac{1}{2}$".
Musée Picasso, Paris
Photo courtesy © R.M.N.

Page 47
Portrait of Daniel-Henry Kahnweiler. 1910
Oil on canvas, $39\frac{5}{8} \times 28\frac{5}{8}$".
The Art Institute of Chicago
Gift of Mrs. Gilbert W. Chapman in memory
of Charles B. Goodspeed
Photo courtesy © 1990 The Art Institute of Chicago

Page 48
Head of a Woman. 1909
Bronze, $16\frac{1}{4} \times 9\frac{3}{4} \times 10\frac{1}{2}$".
Collection, The Museum of Modern Art, New York
Purchase

Page 49
Guitar. 1912–13
Sheet metal and wire, $30\frac{1}{2} \times 13\frac{1}{8} \times 7\frac{5}{8}$".
Collection, The Museum of Modern Art, New York
Gift of the artist

Page 52
Portrait of Olga in an Armchair. 1917
Oil on canvas, $51\frac{1}{8} \times 35$".
Musée Picasso, Paris
Photo courtesy © R.M.N.

Page 53
Harlequin. 1915
Oil on canvas, $6'\frac{1}{4}" \times 41\frac{3}{8}$".
Collection, The Museum of Modern Art, New York
Acquired through the Lillie P. Bliss Bequest

Pages 54–55
Family on the Seashore. 1922
Oil on canvas, $6\frac{15}{16} \times 7\frac{15}{16}$".
Musée Picasso, Paris
Photo courtesy © R.M.N.

Page 56
Three Musicians. 1921
Oil on canvas, 80×74".
Philadelphia Museum of Art
A. E. Gallatin Collection

Page 59
The Kiss. 1925
Oil on canvas, $51\frac{3}{8} \times 38\frac{1}{2}$".
Musée Picasso, Paris
Photo courtesy © R.M.N.

Page 60
Seated Woman. 1927
Oil on wood, $51\frac{1}{8} \times 38\frac{1}{4}$".
Collection, The Museum of Modern Art, New York
Gift of James Thrall Soby

Pages 62–63
The Crucifixion. 1930
Oil on plywood, $20\frac{1}{4} \times 26\frac{1}{8}$".
Musée Picasso, Paris
Photo courtesy © R.M.N.

Page 64
Bust of a Woman. 1931
Bronze, $25\frac{1}{8}$" high.
Musée Picasso, Paris
Photo courtesy © R.M.N.

Page 66
Bull's Head. 1942
Bicycle seat and handlebars, $16\frac{1}{8}$" high.
Musée Picasso, Paris

Pages 67–68
Minotauromachia. 1935
Etching, $19\frac{1}{2} \times 27\frac{7}{16}$".
Collection, The Museum of Modern Art, New York
Purchase fund

Pages 69–71 (gatefold)
Guernica. 1937
Oil on canvas, $11'6" \times 25'8"$.
Prado, Madrid

Page 72
Death's Head. 1943
Casts in bronze and copper
$11\frac{3}{8} \times 8\frac{3}{8} \times 10\frac{1}{4}$".
Musée Picasso, Paris
Photo courtesy © R.M.N.

Pages 73–75 (gatefold)
Bullfight: Death of the Torero. 1933
Oil on wood panel, $12\frac{3}{16} \times 15\frac{3}{4}$".
Musée Picasso, Paris
Photo courtesy © R.M.N.

Page 76
Portrait of Dora Maar. 1937
Oil on canvas, $36\frac{1}{4} \times 25\frac{5}{8}$".
Musée Picasso, Paris
Photo courtesy © R.M.N.

Page 79
Picasso with his second Wife, Jacqueline, and a visitor
© Photo Pic, Paris

Page 80
Baboon and Young. 1951 (cast 1955)
Bronze, $21 \times 13\frac{1}{4} \times 20\frac{3}{4}$".
Collection, The Museum of Modern Art, New York
Mrs. Simon Guggenheim Fund

Page 81
The Charnel House. 1945
Oil and charcoal on canvas, $6'6\frac{5}{8}" \times 8'2\frac{1}{2}"$.
Collection, The Museum of Modern Art, New York

Page 83
Chicago Monument. 1964
Cor-ten steel, 50′ high.
Civic Center Plaza, Chicago

Pages 84–85
La Joie de Vivre (The Joy of Life). 1946
Oil on canvas, $47\frac{1}{4} \times 59$".
Musée Grimaldi, Athens

Pages 86–87
Women of Algiers (After Delacroix). 1955
Oil on canvas, $44\frac{7}{8} \times 57\frac{1}{2}$".
Photo courtesy of Collection Mrs. Victor Ganz
Photographer: Pollitzer, Strong & Meyer

Page 88
The Matador. 1970
Oil on canvas, $57\frac{1}{4} \times 44\frac{7}{8}$".
Musée Picasso, Paris
Photo courtesy © R.M.N.

Index